Introduction to th iPad and iPhone

The iBooks App

© 2018 iTandCoffee

iOS 11 Edition

Special Sales and Supply Queries

For any information about buying this title in bulk quantities, or for supply of this title for educational or fund-raising purposes, contact iTandCoffee on **1300 885 420** or email **enquiry@itandcoffee.com.au**.

iTandCoffee classes and private appointments

For queries about classes and private appointments with iTandCoffee, call **1300 885 420** or email **enquiry@itandcoffee.com.au**.

iTandCoffee operates in and around Glen Iris, Victoria in Australia.

Introducing iTandCoffee ...

iTandCoffee is a Melbourne-based business that was founded in 2012, by IT professional Lynette Coulston.

Lynette and the staff at iTandCoffee have a passion for helping others - especially women of all ages - to enter and navigate the new, and often daunting, world of technology.

At iTandCoffee, **patience is our virtue.**

You'll find a welcoming smile, a relaxed cup of tea or coffee, and a genuine enthusiasm for helping you to gain the confidence to use and enjoy your technology.

With personalised appointments and small, friendly classes – either at our bright, comfortable, cafe-style shop in Glen Iris or at your place - we offer a brand of technology support and education that is so hard to find.

At iTandCoffee, you won't find young 'techies' who speak in a foreign language and move at a pace that leaves you floundering and 'bamboozled'!

Our focus is on helping you to use your technology in a way that enhances your personal and/or professional life – to feel more informed, organised, connected and entertained!

4

iTandCoffee
Relax, we'll help you get iT

Call on iTandCoffee for help with all sorts of technology – Apple, Windows, iCloud, Evernote, Dropbox, all sorts of other Apps (including Microsoft Office products), getting you set up on the internet, setting up a printer, and so much more.

Here are just some of the topics covered in our regular classes at iTandCoffee:

- Introduction to the iPad and iPhone
- The next step on your iPad and iPhone
- Bring your Busy Life under Control using the iPad and iPhone
- Getting to know your Mac
- Understanding and using iCloud
- An Organised Life with Evernote
- Taking and Managing photos on the iPhone and iPad
- Travel with your iPad, iPhone and other technology.
- Keeping kids safe on the iPad, iPhone and iPod Touch.
- Staying Safe Online

The iTandCoffee website (itandcoffee.com.au) offers a wide variety of resources for those brave enough to venture online to learn more: handy hints for iPad, iPhone and Mac; videos and slideshows of iTandCoffee classes; guides on a range of topics; a blog covering all sorts of topical events.

We also produce a regular Handy Hint newsletter full of information that is of interest to our clients and subscribers.

Hopefully, that gives you a bit of a picture of iTandCoffee and what we are about. Please don't hesitate to iTandCoffee on 1300 885 420 to discuss our services or to make a booking.

We hope you enjoy this guide, and find its contents informative and useful. Please feel free to offer feedback at feedback@itandcoffee.com.au.

Regards,

Lynette Coulston (iTandCoffee Owner)

Introduction to the iPad and iPhone

The iBooks App

TABLE OF CONTENTS

Introduction to the iPad and iPhone

The iBooks App

Introduction to the iPad and iPhone

The iBooks App

TABLE OF CONTENTS

Introduction

What is iBooks

The **iBooks** app on the iPad and iPhone allows you to

- read electronic books (i.e. eBooks),
- store and read PDF documents, and
- listen to audiobooks.
- Sample fiction and non-fiction iBooks

iBooks is Apple's equivalent to a Kindle®, or Kobo® eBook reader.

If you already have a Kindle® and purchase books through the Amazon book stores, you might not choose to use iBooks – and instead download the Kindle app if you want to read the books that you have purchased, on your iPad or iPhone instead of the Kindle.

iBooks can only read eBooks in Apples iBooks format.

iBooks is installed as one of the standard apps on the iPad and iPhone – but if you don't have it (or have removed it), the app is available for free download from the **App Store**.

Introducing Collections

Books and PDFs in **iBooks** are grouped into something called **Collections**.

You will see your **Collections** menu at the top centre of the iBooks main screens.

My Books screen on iPad

MyBooks screen on iPhone

Introduction

This 'drop-down' **Collections** Menu contains the following default 'collections' items - **All Books**, **Books**, **Audiobooks**, **PDFs**, **Samples.**

You can also add your own **Collections** to this list. We'll look at how do this later in this guide.

Exploring the main iBooks options

Have you tried reading a book using iBooks on your iPad?

Let's look first at the options along the bottom of the main iBooks screen, as these options will determine what you see elsewhere on the screen.

We will generally focus on what you see on an iPad.

(The key difference for the iPhone is that you don't see the Top Authors option along the bottom and that the 'search' option 🔍 appears in its place.)

If the **My Books** option is selected along the bottom (i.e. it is **blue**), you will see the following options along the top of your iBooks screen.

Show Library as List (with book/file and author name) or as 'book shelves'.

Shows which collection is currently in view – tap to select a different collection

*Tap **Select** to choose items to move between collections, to rename an item, or to delete.*

This symbol will only appear if you have items in your collection that are not yet uploaded to your iCloud.

If **Featured**, **Top Charts** or **Top Authors** is selected, the options along the top of the screen will be as follows.

View iBooks Store content for a chosen Category

View iBooks or Audiobooks (not visible for Top Authors)

Search the iBooks store by title or author

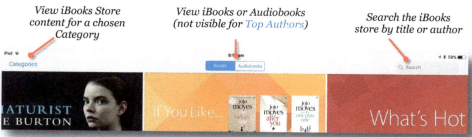

The **Purchased** option shows all purchases made from the iBooks store.

Getting an iBook

If you have not previously used iBooks, you will find your iBooks bookshelf is empty when you open the iBooks app!

This can be quickly remedied by a visit to the iBooks store, where you can purchase both free and paid iBooks.

You can even download a 'sample' – the first few chapters - of a book, to 'try before you buy'.

Where is the iBooks store app?

Unlike the iTunes Store and The App Store, the iBooks store is not a separate App.

The iBooks store is accessed from within your **iBooks** app.

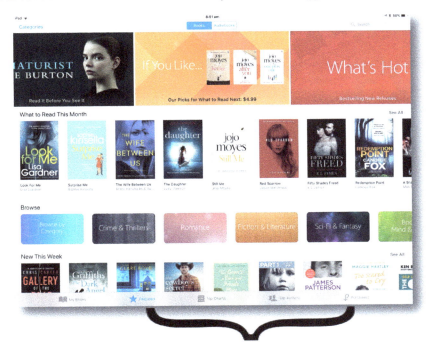

The rightmost four options provided at the bottom of the main iBooks screen - **Featured, Top Charts, Top Authors** and **Purchased** – represent your **iBooks** store.

The **My Books** option on the left shows the books that you have already purchased and PDFs that you have saved to iBooks – i.e. that are in your iBooks Library.

Getting an iBook

But I can't see any 'store' options!

When the **iBooks** app is opened, the screen that you first see will reflect what you were last doing in the iBooks app - whether you were visiting the iBooks Store, viewing your Library or reading a book.

If you have **a book currently open,** you will see a blue arrow < at top left.

Touch on this to return to the view that shows your iBooks Library and the Store options.

Shopping for iBooks

You will find many aspects of the iBooks store similar to the **iTunes** store – with **Featured**, **Top Charts**, and **Purchased** options, and with the **Categories** options at the top left (similar to **Genres** in iTunes). In the iBooks store, there is the additional option to browse **Top Authors**.

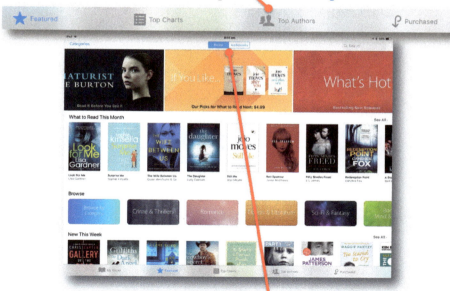

Choose at the top middle whether you wish to shop for **Books** or **Audiobooks**.

Getting an iBook

Featured

Featured allows you to peruse a selection of books that Apple has chosen to feature – and this changes on a regular basis. (See previous image for an example of the **Featured** screen.)

Top Charts

Top Charts has a long list of free books – especially the classics! And you can see what books are the most popular at the moment. On the iPad, 'Paid' books are on the left, and 'Free' are on the right. On the iPhone, Paid books are shown first – scroll down for Free.

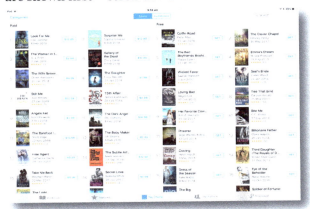
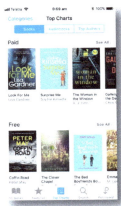

Top Authors

Top Authors provides the options to view either **Paid** or **Free** books, listing all authors in alphabetical order. On the iPhone, you find the **Top Authors** by tapping **Top Charts** and choosing the option at the top.

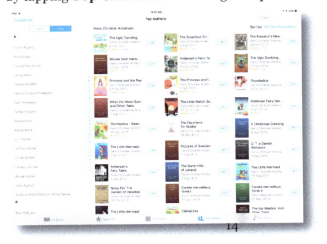

14

Getting an iBook

On the top right of the iPad when looking at **Top Authors**, you will have the option to **Sort by:** and can choose **All-Time Bestsellers**, **Name** or **Release Date**.

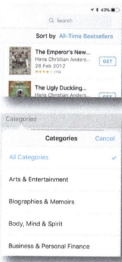

Categories

The Categories option at top left is available on the **Featured**, **Top Charts** and **Top Authors** screens.

Tap Categories and choose what type of books or audiobooks you would like to browse (or choose **All Categories** if you don't want to filter on Category.

You will see quite a long list of options to choose from.

Search

Use the **Search** field at the top right on the iPad to look for a specific author or title.

On the iPhone, the **Search** option is in the bottom toolbar. Tapping this option provides a search bar at the top – tap that bar and type your search phrase.

Sample a book

If you see a book that is of interest, you can download a sample of the book to see if it meets your fancy! Just tap on the image of the book to see further details about it, then choose the SAMPLE option (instead of tapping on the price).

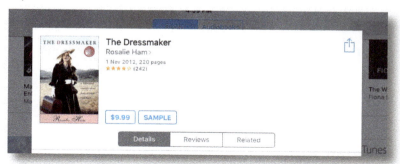

Getting an iBook

When you return to your Library by tapping My Books, you will see the book that you just chose to Sample – with a tag at the top right showing it is just a sample of the book.

This will give you the first few chapters of the book – just to 'whet your whistle' - and decide if you really want to spend any money on it.

If you like a book, buy it!

To buy a book you see in the iBooks store, just tap the price and follow the prompts to download it to your iBooks library. Once downloaded, you will see it on you **My Books** library, in your **All Books** and **Books** Collections.

We won't go into the details in this guide about browsing the iBooks store and purchasing from this store.

If you need further information about purchasing content for your iPad or iPhone (including setting up an Apple ID to allow such purchasing) check out another iTandCoffee Guide, **Shopping the Stores – Apps, Movies, Music, Books, Podcasts (iOS 11)**.

Getting Audiobooks

I love a good Audiobook. One of my all-time favourites was 'The Help' – a beautifully read audiobook, with different voices for the different characters.

Audiobooks are great listening when you travel, when you walk, or just want to unwind.

There is a wide range of books available through iTunes – although many people choose to use **Amazon** and its app **Audible** for purchasing and listening to Audiobooks., as this can work out cheaper than iBooks.

You will find that audiobooks can often be quite expensive when compared to standard iBooks.

Just make sure that you **Preview** the book before you buy!

The voice of the reader can honestly make or break an Audiobook, so make sure you like that voice before spending any money.

Reading a Book

Viewing your Library

To start reading using iBooks, touch on the iBooks app on your Home screen.

If you find that, on opening, the iBooks app is showing the content of the iBook (or a PDF) that you most recently had open, tap the < at top left to return to the main iBooks screen.

You will then (hopefully) see your Bookshelf (or a list) of books that you have already purchased, downloaded or saved to your iBooks app.

If you do not see the books you have already purchased/downloaded, make sure you are viewing your **My Books** option at bottom left (as described earlier).

We'll talk further shortly about the bookshelf, the alternative 'list' view, and about different types of 'books'.

We'll also look at how you can easily move items between your Collections of books and PDFS, and re-arrange within these Collections.

First though, let's look at reading an individual iBook.

Reading a Book

Open a Book or PDF

To open an iBook in your iBooks library, just tap on it once.

Your screen will initially show the book with options at the top and bottom.

An important option to note is the < option at the top left.

Touch on this at any time to leave your book and return to the iBooks library.

To make the top and bottom options disappear - so that you just see the book's contents – just touch once in the middle of the screen.

To make these options come back again when all you can see is your book, just tap the middle of the screen again.

Viewing your Book or PDF

If you are viewing an iBook, the 'look' of your screen will depend on your iPad's orientation. The first example above right shows an iBook on an iPad or iPhone that is in 'portrait' orientation.

If your iPad is in 'landscape' orientation on the iPad, your iBook will look something like the image below. (Note. PDF's always show as a single page.) Whether you view your book in portrait or landscape orientation in your iPad is really just a matter of preference.

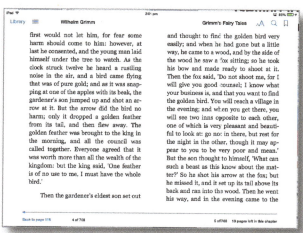

Reading a Book

Move from page to page

Moving between pages of your iBook or PDF on your iPad and iPhone easy – as with a 'real' book, you can just 'flick' through your pages.

To go to the next page of a book, just drag or swipe you finger from right to left across the screen

To go back to a previous page, just swipe in the other direction – left-to-right.

Alternatively, just **tap in the right margin** to go to the next page.

Or **tap in the left margin** to go to the previous page.

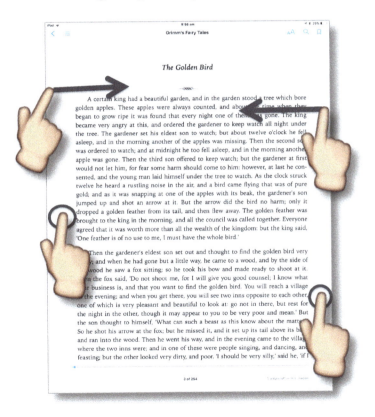

Reading a Book

View a summary of the contents of an iBook

If you have the options at the top of your screen in view, you will notice a symbol at the top left.

(If you don't see any options at the moment, just tap on the middle of the screen to make these options appear.)

Touch on ☷ to view a summary of the contents of your book or document.

Make sure that the **Contents** option is shaded – if it isn't, touch on **Contents** so that it becomes the active view. (We'll talk about the other options that you see here shortly.)

If you are viewing an iBook, this option will show you the chapters of your book and allow you to touch on an individual chapter to go directly to it.

Swipe up and down to view the full list of sections or chapters.

When you have finished with this view and want to return to the book, you can touch **Resume** at the top right.

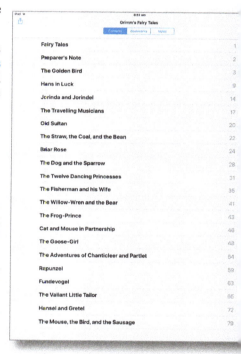

Reading a Book

View a summary of the contents of a PDF

If the document you are viewing is a PDF, choose the ▤ option to view a summary of the document in the form of 'thumbnails' of the its. (Remember, if you don't see the options at the top of the screen, tap in the middle of the screen to make them appear.)

Once again, drag or swipe up and down to view the full set of pages.

Touch on any page to go directly to that page in the document.

When you have finished with this view and want to return to viewing the pages of the document, touch Resume (top left).

You will be returned to the page that you were last viewing.

Reading a Book

Moving to a different part of the iBook or PDF

When you have the blue options available at the top of the screen (tap the centre of the screen if are not seeing them at the moment), you may also notice a 'bar' at the bottom of the screen.

The way this bar looks will depend on whether you are looking at an iBook or PDF.

For a book, the bar will be in the form of a 'slider'. Hold your finger on the blue dot on this slider and drag your finger to the right and left to move through the pages of the book.

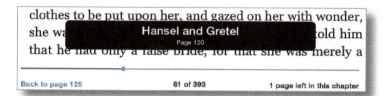

A black box will show the page number that the 'dot' is positioned at, along with chapter details. Just lift your finger from the screen when you find the page that you need – you will be positioned at that page.

For a PDF, the bar at the bottom of the screen will show a row of tiny thumbnails of the pages in your document.

Drag your finger along this row of thumbnails to see a preview of each page, or just touch on a thumbnail to go directly to that page.

Reading a Book

When you've finished reading ...

When you have finished with your book (either just for now, or you have reached the end), return to your Library by touching < at the top left.

If you don't see this symbol at top left, touch in the middle of the screen to make it appear again.

This will take you back to your bookshelf (or list) of books and/or PDF documents, to allow you to select another.

If you have just finished reading for now and want to be able to continue reading the book next time you return to the iBooks app, just press the Home button to return you your Home Screen.

Your book will be ready and waiting for you when you next select the iBooks app. When you touch on iBooks from your Home Screen again, you will go straight back to your book, right back to the page that you were last reading.

Even if you had returned to your Library before exiting iBooks, when you next select that same book from the bookshelf, you will find yourself returned to the page that you were last reading. iBooks remembers where you were up to.

If you have chosen to 'sync' your iBooks using iCloud, you can resume your reading on any device – as your position in the book is known to each of your iCloud-connected devices.

Customising your iBook

One of the best things about reading iBooks on your iPad or iPhone is that you have the ability to adjust the way your book looks – to change the text size and font style, adjust brightness, and even choose the colour of your background.

All of these features of your book can by adjusted from the option at the top right of the screen when you are reading a book.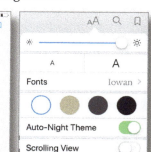

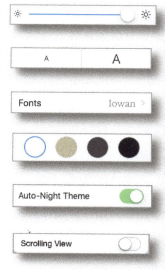

(This set of options is only available if you are viewing an iBook - but not for a PDF.)

To adjust the brightness of your book's screen, adjust the top slider (i.e. drag the dot to adjust).

To adjust the size of the book's text, touch one or more times on either the large 'A' (to increase the text size) or the small 'A' (to decrease the text size).

Choose the font if you would rather a different font to what you see.

Choose the background for your book's pages using the colour selector.

Choose for your iPad to automatically switch to **Night Theme** (black background and white text) to cut down on screen glare when the sun is down

You can also choose whether you prefer to 'flick' through your book's pages or whether you want to read by just scrolling down through the pages.

Discover Markup for PDFs

You won't see the same AA option when viewing a PDF.

Instead, you have the wonderful Ⓐ option (top right) that you can use to 'markup' a PDF that you have received – perhaps a document that you need to review and provide feedback.

Activating Markup

Tapping Ⓐ will provide a set of editing options along the bottom of the screen.

Choose your pen

Markup allows you to write or draw on a PDF (or image), using a set of pens that are provided along the bottom of the screen. Tap on the type/ thickness of pen/pencil you need and use your finger, stylus or Apple Pencil to draw or write on the screen.

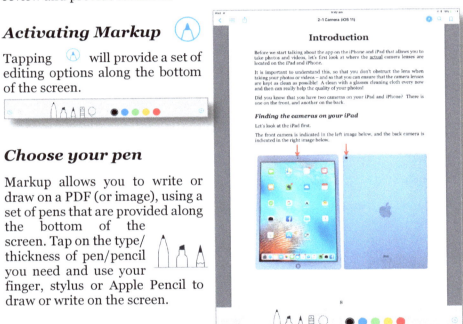

Rub out your mistakes

There is an Eraser to 'rub out' anything you have added. Tap the eraser symbol to activate this feature (then tap a pen/pencil to deactivate it).

Choose a colour

A colour palette is provided at the bottom – tap any colour to choose the colour of your pen or pencil.

Discover Markup for PDFs

Move your markups

If you have marked up your PDF, and you need to move something you added to a different position, use the 'lasso'. Tap this symbol, then draw a circle around the markup that you wish to move. You will see a 'dotted circle' around the markup. Drag the circled area to its new location.

Tap another option to deactivate the 'lasso' option.

Discovering more markup options

There are further markup options that can be uncovered by tapping the ⊕ symbol at bottom right.

- Add a text box to type some test,

- Create/add a signature (which you can store for future use and easily sign documents electronically) – so handy if you don't have a printer/scanner and need to sign a document to send to someone.

- Add a 'magnifier' to highlight a part of the page, or add shape objects

- Add a shape or arrow.

We won't go into these in further detail here, as they are covered elsewhere in iTandCoffee guides and in iTandCoffee's Handy Hints library.

Searching your book

The iBooks app allows you to perform a search of the iBook or PDF that you are reading – for example, to look for a particular word, quote or page number.

(Note. Not all PDF's can be searched for text. Only PDF's generated from a text document can be searched in the iBooks app.)

Just touch on the 'Search' symbol 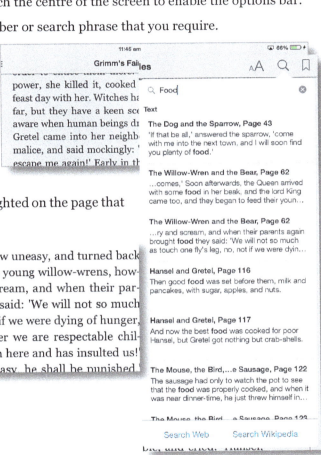 at the top right of the screen – if you don't see this symbol, touch the centre of the screen to enable the options bar.

Then, enter the page number or search phrase that you require.

A list of pages and phrases that match your search criteria will be shown.

Touch on the required item in the list to go to that page or paragraph.

The search phrase that you entered will be highlighted on the page that you are taken to.

The bear and the wolf grew uneasy, and turned back nd went into their holes. The young willow-wrens, how-ver, continued to cry and scream, and when their par-ts again brought food they said: 'We will not so much s touch one fly's leg, no, not if we were dying of hunger, ntil you have settled whether we are respectable chil-ren or not; the bear has been here and has insulted us!' hen the old King said: 'Be easy, he shall be punished.

Bookmarking your book

Creating a bookmark

There are times, when reading an iBook or PDF, that you will want to make note of a page so that you can come back to it later.

iBooks has a feature call 'Bookmarking' that allows you to easily tag those pages that you want keep track of and re-visit.

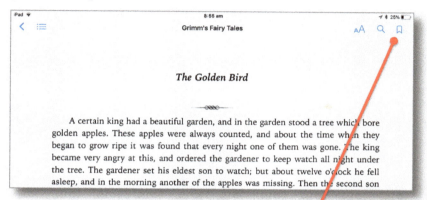

When positioned at a page that you want to 'Bookmark', just tap on the Bookmark symbol ⌐ at the top right of the screen.

You will see the bookmark symbol change to red ▮, thereby indicating that the page has now been bookmarked.

Removing a Bookmark

To remove a bookmark that you no longer need, just touch on the red bookmark ▮ – it will change back to the 'outline-only' ⌐ symbol to show that the page is no longer bookmarked.

Finding the pages you have Bookmarked?

Just touch on ☰ at the top left to view a list of all of your Bookmarks, choose a particular bookmark or to manage/remove your bookmarks.

If you don't see ☰, tap on the middle of the screen to make it appear. (Of course, you must be reading a particular book for this to work.)

Bookmarking your book

The screen that we previously looked at for the Table of Contents will appear when your touch ☰ .

This time, touch on the Bookmarks option in the middle so that its background is shaded blue.

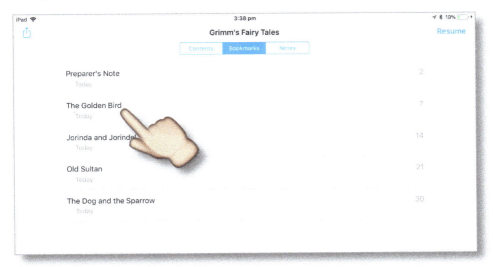

Your set of bookmarks will be listed. To go to a particular Bookmark, just touch on it.

To clean up Bookmarks that you no longer need, swipe from right to left across that bookmark to reveal the **Delete** option.

Tap **Delete** to remove the Bookmark.

Annotating your iBook

Now, here's a great feature for anyone wanting to record notes about the iBook they are reading.

iBooks allows you to annotate iBooks by highlighting areas of text in a colour, and even recording some notes about the text that has been highlighted!

You can choose what colour you would like to use for your highlighting, and perhaps even share the highlighted text in an email or text!

So how is this done?

Selecting text to annotate

Just use the techniques you learned earlier in the **Typing and Editing** guide so select an area of text.

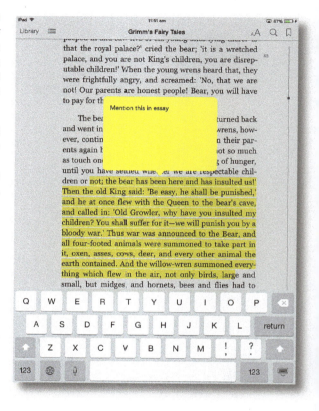

Double-tap on a word so that you have an area of shaded blue with dots at either end. Then, 'spread' the blue dots to select the required text.

When you release your finger, you will see a series of options pop up above the selected text – Speak (optional), Copy, Highlight, Note, Search, Share.

Annotating your iBook

Highlight some text

To highlight the selected text with a particular colour, just touch **Highlight**, then touch the set of dots on the left.

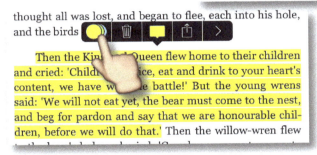

Choose the required colour (if you want a different colour to the default provided).

Underline Text

You can even choose to underline the text instead of highlighting it, by choosing the 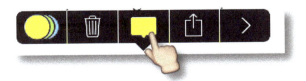 symbol (rightmost 'dot' above).

Record a note about some text

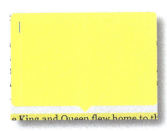

To type a note about the selected area of text, touch on Note symbol in the black bar that appears when you tap **Highlight** in the black bar.

If you don't see this option (ie you are just seeing your highlighted text without any option bar) , just touch on the area of text that is highlighted to see the bar.

Type your note in the 'speech bubble' that appears.

Annotating your iBook

Share your notation (and the selected text)

To share the selected area of text in an email or text, touch the Share option.

Remove an annotation

To remove highlighting or a note that you have previously added, just touch on the area of text so that the black bar appears above the text, then touch on the trash can 🗑 to remove the highlighting and/or the note.

View your list of annotation

To view a list of all your notes and highlighted text, touch on ☰ at the top left.

Touch on the **Notes** option at the top. Your highlighted text and any notes will be listed. From here, you can select one or more notes and 'Share' them by email.

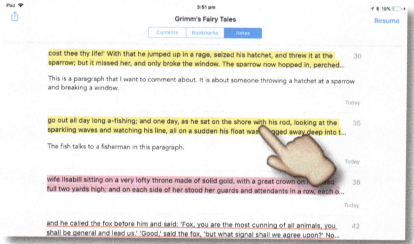

Or just touch on a note to go to the corresponding page in the document.

Delete an annotation from Notes

Once again, swipe from right-to-left across a note to see the **Delete** option – touch this option to remove the highlighting and/or note.

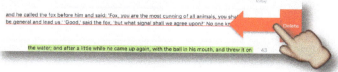

Annotating your iBook

Share all your annotations and selected text

Wouldn't it be great if you could get all your annotations, notes and the full selected text associated with them, in one list?

You will see that the **Notes** (accessed by tapping the ☰ option) only shows you two lines of the text that you have selected, meaning that you need to tap on the note to visit the page and see the full text selection.

Here is how to produce a **full list of your annotations, selected text and notes**.

Tap the Share symbol ⬆️ at top left while viewing your list of **Notes**.

You will see the options **Share Book** and **Edit Notes**.

Choose **Edit Notes**.

At the top left is the option **Select All** – choose this to select ALL your Notes, or tap the circles on the left of items in the list to select only certain items.

Choose **Share** (which will be at top left), then the **Mail** option.

You will see a draft email that shows the list of text selections and any notes that you made! Send this to yourself to have all your Notes!

Browsing your collection of books

The Bookshelf view of your library allows you to browse your books and PDFs.

Your books are lined up in across your screen in rows - scroll up and down to view you full set of books.

You can also choose instead to view your books in a list format.

When you are viewing your bookshelves of books, touch on ≡ at the top left of the screen to switch to the 'list' view of your collection of books.

Your 'shelves' of books will turn into a list, showing the names of each item and, if available, the author. For PDFs you will see the file name – and, depending on the PDF, you may also see an Author.

Browsing your collection of books

When in 'list' view, you will have some 'sort' options along the top of the screen.

These options will allow you to view your books in different orders – by Title, by Author, or by Category.

Categories will group your books according to categories like **Contemporary**, **Crime & Thrillers**, and **Fiction & Literature**

If you are in your **All Books** category, the leftmost option will be Most Recent, showing your iBooks/PDFs in the order you last accessed or added them.

If you are looking at any other Collection (which we will describe further shortly), you will see the option Bookshelf as the leftmost option.

This allows you to see your books in the order they appear in your Bookshelf – an order that you can re-arrange. We'll cover this a bit later.

To return you the 'Bookshelf' view, just touch ⊞ at the top left of the screen.

Organising your Library - Collections

The iBooks and PDFs in your iBooks library can be organized into groups called Collections.

For example, you could create a Collection that contains all the PDF documents that you have saved from your emails – perhaps even have a Collection that just contains your Bank Statements or Electricity bills.

If you have some children's books on your iPad, these could be grouped into a Children's Books collection.

The standard Collections

There are 5 standard Collections:

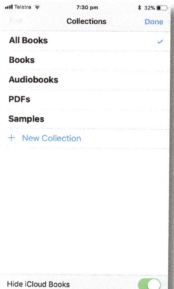

All Books: Shows all iBooks, PDFs, Audiobook, and Samples, sorted by date added/last viewed.
Books: Shows only iBooks (including Samples).
PDFs: Shows only PDFs.
Audiobooks: Shows only audiobooks
Samples – Shows the sample iBooks you have downloaded.

In all Collections but **All Books**, the order in which the items appear can be re-arranged to suit your requirements.

To create a new Collection

While viewing your Library, touch on whatever Collections option appears at the top middle of the screen (reflecting the name of the Collection that you are currently viewing).

A list of all your current Collections will show.

To create a new collection, just touch on the final option in the list, + New Collection.

Your keyboard will appear – just type in the name for the new Collection.

Your new Collection will appear at the end of the list, just above the + New Collection option. This new Collection can contain either Books, PDFs, or both.

Organising your Library - Collections

Move an iBook or PDF to a collection

Go to the bookshelf and tap **Select** at the top right.

Tap to select the items you want to move – a blue circle with a tick will appear on each item that has been selected.

Touch on **Move** at top left.

Then, choose (tap) the **Collection** into which the selected items are to be moved.

You can even choose to create a + New Collection at this point using the last option in the list.

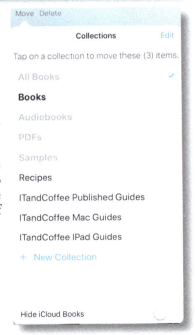

The selected items will go into that New Collection (or the selected existing Collection)

You might notice that there are sometimes 'greyed' options in the list when you want to select a Collection. This is because these are the Collections that relate to a different type of library content.

Organising your Library - Collections

View the books in a particular Collection

To view the books that belong to a particular collection (one that is not currently in view), touch on the **Collection** that appears at top middle, and then touch on the required **Collection** from the list.

Alternatively, when viewing your shelf/list of books in the library, just swipe left to right or right to left to move through your different Collections.

If you keep swiping, you will find that you cycle through all of your Collections and start again.

Organising your Library - Collections

Deleting a Collection

Any collection that you no longer need can be deleted.

Touch on the Collections Menu at the top of screen, then touch Edit at top right of that list.

Your list of Collections will appear in **Edit** mode, with a red circle on the left.

Touch on  to delete any Collection you no longer require.

Tap Delete (which appears on the right) to confirm that you want to delete the Collection.

You will be asked if the contents of the Collection should be removed from the device when the Collection is deleted.

Delete Collection?

If you delete the collection only, its books will return to the Books collection.

Delete Collection and Content

Delete Collection Only

Cancel

If you choose **not** to remove the contents, they will be returned to their original Collection based on the type of each item – Books, PDFs, or Audiobooks.

Touch Done (top right of the Collections list) when finished.

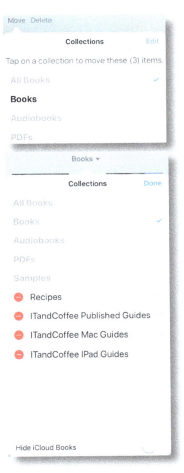

Organising your Library - Collections

Change the order of your collections

Open your Collections by tapping on the Collections Menu at top middle of screen.

Touch and hold on ▬▬ and drag up or down to change the order of the Collections.

Touch **Done** when finished.

Changing the name of a collection

Once again, open your list of Collections by tapping on the Collections menu at top middle of screen.

Choose **Edit** at top right of the Collections list.

Touch on the name of the Collection that needs its name changed.

You will then be in 'edit' mode, allowing the name to be changed.

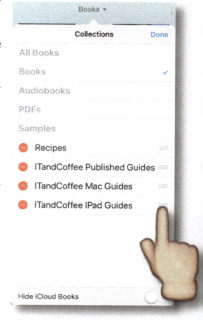

Use backspace and standard editing techniques to remove/change the previous name and type a new name.

When you are finished, touch on **Done**.

Managing Books in a Collection

Delete books

Books that you have purchased are available any time from the iBooks store (to re-download for free), so there is no problem with occasionally doing a clean-out of the iBooks library!

In fact, this may help to reduce data usage on your device.

To delete books from your library, just touch Select at the top right of the screen (from your **My Books** view in iBooks).

Touch on the items/s that you want to delete.

A tick will appear on the selected item/s.

Then just touch Delete at the top left. A confirmation message will appear – choose Delete again to confirm.

Managing Books in a Collection

Change the order of books in the bookshelf

If you are in the Bookshelf view of any collection other than **All Books**, touch and hold an item in the bookshelf, then drag it to its new position.

(The **All Books** collection is sorted by date last opened, and can't be re-ordered.)

If you are in the 'list' view of any collection other than **All Books**, tap Select at top right.

Then touch and drag the ≡ on right of the item that you want to move up or down. Drag it up or down to the required new position.

Search for a book

Drag down from the top of the screen, then tap in the field Q Search .

Type in your search phrase – a book/file name, author or category.

Download a book from iCloud

Books you've purchased that aren't on your iPad (or iPhone) appear with an iCloud badge in the top right corner.

To download the book, tap this iCloud symbol.

Managing Books in a Collection

Hide iCloud Books

You can choose to show or hide purchased books that aren't currently on your iPad or iPhone. This can help to keep your bookshelf from being cluttered with books you have already read and removed.

Go to the Collections Menu (by tapping the Collection showing at top middle of the screen) and push the slider at the bottom of the Collections list to either On or Off, depending on your preference.

Automatically download items purchased on other devices

Go to **Settings > iTunes & App Store**.

In the **Automatic Downloads** section, slide **Books & Audiobooks** to 'On'.

This will ensure that any iBooks you purchase on another device will be downloaded to this device as well.

Sharing or printing from iBooks

Choose the share option ⬆️ in iBooks, to elect to email or (in some cases) to print it.

(This option is not visible in all cases.)

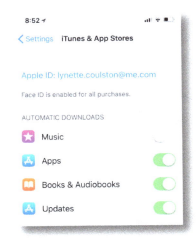

Saving a PDF to iBooks

Throughout this guide, mention has been made many times about viewing and managing PDFs in iBooks.

But how do these PDFs get into iBooks in the first place?

Saving PDF from a Mail message

If you see a PDF in as an attachment in an email,

1. Just touch on that PDF and it will open and show its contents.

2. Once you have the PDF open on your screen, touch on the 'Share' symbol ⬆ .

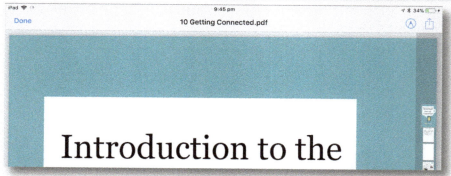

3. Choose the **Copy to iBooks** option to get that document into your iBooks.

Saving a PDF to iBooks

Save PDF from an application other than mail

1. Save a PDF from another application by touching the Share symbol

2. If you see the **Open in iBooks or Copy to iBooks** option, touch on this to save the PDF to iBooks and open it in iBooks.

3. If you don't see one of these options, but you see the 'Open in' option, touch on this.

4. You will then see a list of options for Apps where the PDF can be saved. The list you see here will depend on what Apps you have installed on your iPad or iPhone. If you see an option relating to iBooks in this list, turn it on.

5. Once in iBooks, you can then put your document in to the required Collection for easy retrieval next time you need it.

Other Guides in the **Introduction to the iPad and iPhone** Series

iTandCoffee has a wide range of guides about the iPad and iPhone, covering topics like

* **A Guided Tour**
* **The Camera App**
* **The Photos App**
* **Typing and Editing**
* **The Mail App**
* **The Calendar App**
* **The Phone App**
* **Shopping the Stores**
* **Discovering iBooks**
* **Getting Connected**
* **And more**

Visit www.itandcoffee.com.au/guides for more information.